How To Use This Study Guide

This five-lesson study guide corresponds to *"The Baptism in the Holy Spirit" With Rick Renner* (Renner TV). Each lesson in this study guide covers a topic that is addressed during the program series, with questions and references supplied to draw you deeper into your own private study of the Scriptures on this subject.

To derive the most benefit from this study guide, consider the following:

First, watch or listen to the program prior to working through the corresponding lesson in this guide. (Programs can also be viewed at **renner.org** by clicking on the Media/Archives links or on our Renner Ministries YouTube channel.)

Second, take the time to look up the scriptures included in each lesson. Prayerfully consider their application to your own life.

Third, use a journal or notebook to make note of your answers to each lesson's Study Questions and Practical Application challenges.

Fourth, invest specific time in prayer and in the Word of God to consult with the Holy Spirit. Write down the scriptures or insights He reveals to you.

Finally, take action! Whatever the Lord tells you to do according to His Word, do it.

For added insights on this subject, it is recommended that you obtain Rick Renner's book *The Holy Spirit and You: Working Together as Heaven's 'Dynamic Duo.'* You may also select from Rick's other available resources by placing your order at **renner.org** or by calling 1-800-742-5593.

TOPIC

Power To Overcome Evil

SCRIPTURES

1. **Matthew 3:11** — I indeed baptize you with water unto repentance: but he that cometh after me is mightier than I, whose shoes I am not worthy to bear: he shall baptize you with the Holy Ghost, and with fire.

2. **Matthew 3:13** — Then cometh Jesus from Galilee to Jordan unto John, to be baptized of him.

3. **Matthew 3:16** — And Jesus, when he was baptized, went up straightway out of the water: and, lo, the heavens were opened unto him, and he saw the Spirit of God descending like a dove, and lighting upon him.

4. **Matthew 4:1,2** — Then was Jesus led up of the Spirit into the wilderness to be tempted of the devil. And when he had fasted forty days and forty nights, he was afterward an hungred.

5. **Mark 1:7-10,12,13** — And preached, saying, There cometh one mightier than I after me, the latchet of whose shoes I am not worthy to stoop down and unloose. I indeed have baptized you with water: but he shall baptize you with the Holy Ghost. And it came to pass in those days, that Jesus came from Nazareth of Galilee, and was baptized of John in Jordan. And straightway coming up out of the water, he saw the heavens opened, and the Spirit like a dove descending upon him.... And immediately the Spirit driveth him into the wilderness. And he was there in the wilderness forty days, tempted of Satan; and was with the wild beasts....

6. **Luke 3:16** — John answered, saying unto them all, I indeed baptize you with water; but one mightier than I cometh, the latchet of whose shoes I am not worthy to unloose: he shall baptize you with the Holy Ghost and with fire.

7. **Luke 3:21,22** — Now when all the people were baptized, it came to pass, that Jesus also being baptized, and praying, the heaven was

A Note From Rick Renner

I am on a personal quest to see a "revival of the Bible" so people can establish their lives on a firm foundation that will stand strong and endure the test as end-time storm winds begin to intensify.

In order to experience a revival of the Bible in your personal life, it is important to take time each day to read, receive, and apply its truths to your life. James tells us that if we will continue in the perfect law of liberty — refusing to be forgetful hearers, but determined to be doers — we will be blessed in our ways. As you watch or listen to the programs in this series and work through this corresponding study guide, I trust you will search the Scriptures and allow the Holy Spirit to help you hear something new from God's Word that applies specifically to your life. I encourage you to be a doer of the Word He reveals to you. Whatever the cost, I assure you — it will be worth it.

> Thy words were found, and I did eat them;
> and thy word was unto me the joy and rejoicing of mine heart:
> for I am called by thy name, O Lord God of hosts.
> — Jeremiah 15:16

Your brother and friend in Jesus Christ,

Rick Renner

The Baptism in the Holy Spirit

Copyright © 2019 by Rick Renner
1814 W. Tacoma St.
Broken Arrow, OK 74012-1406

Published by Rick Renner Ministries
www.renner.org

ISBN 13: 978-1-6675-1368-3

ISBN 13 eBook: 978-1-6675-1369-0

opened. And the Holy Ghost descended in a bodily shape like a dove upon him….

8. **Luke 4:1,2** — And Jesus being full of the Holy Ghost returned from Jordan, and was led by the Spirit into the wilderness, being forty days tempted of the devil. And in those days he did eat nothing: and when they were ended, he afterward hungered.

9. **Luke 4:14,15** — And Jesus returned in the power of the Spirit into Galilee: and there went out a fame of him through all the region round about. And he taught in their synagogues, being glorified of all.

GREEK WORDS

1. "baptize" — βαπτίζω (*baptidzo*): a word that originally meant to dip and dye; in early usage, it described the process of dipping a cloth or garment into a vat of color to dye it, leaving it there long enough for the material to soak up the new color, and then pulling that garment out of the dye with a permanently changed outward appearance; to baptize; to fully immerse

2. "lo" — ἰδοὺ (*idou*): to behold; pictures shock or amazement; to be stunned; portrays the idea of wow!

3. "like" — ὡσεὶ (*husei*): not like, but as

4. "upon" — ἐπί (*epi*): upon; on

5. "led up" — ἀνάγω (*anago*): I to lead up; to lead from a lower place to a higher place

6. "wilderness" — ἐρημία (*eremia*): a remote, isolated location in the middle of nowhere; a remote place that is out of the way; somewhere off the beaten track; an obscure site or an unfrequented location; such places were often encountered when one traveled by foot, and they often proved to be dangerous because there was little water and no sustenance

7. "tempted" — πειράζω (*peiradzo*): to put to the test; to test in order to prove; to test in order to expose the truth about the quality of a substance; pictures a test designed to expose deficiencies or the trustworthiness of a person or object

8. "devil" — διάβολος (*diabolos*): devil; characteristic of the devil, one who repetitiously strikes until successfully penetrating an object in order to ruin it, affect it, or take it captive

9. "hungred" — πεινάω (*peinao*): pictures extreme hunger; to be famished
10. "driveth" — ἐκβάλλω (*ekballo*): to hurl; to throw out
11. "Satan" — Σατανᾶς (*Satanas*): Satan; the devil; one who hates, accuses, slanders, or conspires against; the adversary
12. "wild beasts" — θηρίον (*therion*): a wild beast; a dangerous animal; pictures vicious killers
13. "full" — πλήρης (*pleres*): full; complete; lacking nothing
14. "nothing" — οὐδὲν (*ouden*): absolutely nothing; emphatically nothing
15. "power" — δύναμις (*dunamis*): power; explosive, superhuman power that comes with enormous energy and produces phenomenal, extraordinary, and unparalleled results; depicts "mighty deeds" that are impressive, incomparable, and beyond human ability to perform; miraculous power or miraculous manifestations

SYNOPSIS

The five lessons in this study on *The Baptism in the Holy Spirit* will focus on the following topics:

• Power To Overcome Evil
• Power To Minister to Others
• Power for Every Believer
• Power To Move Into the Supernatural
• Questions About the Baptism in the Holy Spirit

The emphasis of this lesson:

When you receive the baptism in the Holy Spirit, you receive supernatural power to overcome evil. Jesus proved this during His time of testing in the wilderness.

The Judean wilderness is not too far from the Jordan River where Jesus was baptized by John. It was into this wilderness that the Holy Spirit led Jesus, who was tempted of the devil for 40 days and nights. During that time, Jesus fasted, and at the end of it, He became weak and was extremely hungry. Yet in spite of His physical condition, Jesus didn't cave in to the enemy's allurements. He remained faithful to the Father through the power of the Holy Spirit with whom He had been baptized.

John Identified Jesus as the Baptizer

John the Baptist was the forerunner for Jesus who was sent to prepare the way by preparing people's hearts to receive what the Lord was bringing to earth — salvation through His Son and the redemption of mankind. In Matthew 3:11, John told the crowds, "I indeed baptize you with water unto repentance: but he that cometh after me is mightier than I, whose shoes I am not worthy to bear: he shall baptize you with the Holy Ghost, and with fire"

The word "baptize" in Matthew 3:11 is the Greek word *baptidzo*, which means *to baptize; to fully immerse*. Originally, it meant *to dip and dye. In early usage, it described the process of dipping a cloth or garment into a vat of color to dye it, leaving it there long enough for the material to soak up the new color, and then pulling that garment out of the dye with a permanently changed outward appearance.*

When the Holy Spirit baptized you into Christ in the new birth, you were placed into Christ, and you "emerged" a new creature in Christ (*see* 2 Corinthians 5:17). Subsequent to that experience, there is another baptism God desires that you experience: the baptism in the Holy Spirit. When Jesus baptizes you in the Holy Spirit, He immerses you deeply in His Spirit. He allows you to become so saturated in Him that when you come out, you are infused with His power to live a Spirit-filled, Spirit-led life of victory on earth in the face of every dark challenge and obstacle.

Jesus Was Baptized and Then Led by the Spirit Into the Wilderness

When Jesus was baptized in water by John the Baptist, He was simultaneously baptized with the Holy Spirit. Matthew 3:13 says, "Then cometh Jesus from Galilee to Jordan unto John, to be baptized of him." Verse 16 says, "And Jesus, when he was baptized, went up straightway out of the water: and, lo, the heavens were opened unto him, and he saw the Spirit of God descending like a dove, and lighting upon him."

Interestingly, the word "lo," which is the Greek word *idou*, means *to behold*. It pictures *shock or amazement* and portrays the idea of, *Wow!* It means *to be stunned*. When those who were present at Jesus' baptism saw what was happening, they were in awe. The Holy Spirit descended "like" a dove. This word "like" is the Greek word *husei*, which actually means *as*. This signifies that when the Holy Spirit came "upon" Jesus, His characteristics were *as a dove* — very *gentle in nature*. The word "upon" is the Greek word *epi*, which means *on*, and it indicates that the Spirit rested on Jesus.

After being baptized, the Bible says, "Then was Jesus led up of the Spirit into the wilderness to be tempted of the devil. And when he had fasted forty days and forty nights, he was afterward an hungred" (Matthew 4:1,2). The phrase "led up" is the Greek word *anago*, which means *to lead up; to lead from a lower place to a higher place*. Not only was the Holy Spirit leading Jesus geographically from the lower region of the Jordan River to the higher region of the wilderness, but the Spirit was also taking Jesus from a lower to a higher realm spiritually.

The word "wilderness" in this verse is the Greek word *eremia*. It describes *a remote, isolated location in the middle of nowhere; a remote place that is out of the way; somewhere off the beaten path*. This was *an obscure site or an unfrequented location*. Such places were often encountered when one traveled by foot, and they often proved to be dangerous because there was little water and no sustenance.

The "wilderness" is where the Holy Spirit led Jesus, and He did it so that Jesus could be "tempted of the devil." The word "tempted" is the Greek word *peiradzo*, which means *to put to the test; to test in order to prove; to test in order to expose the truth about the quality of a substance*. This word *peiradzo* pictures *a test designed to expose deficiencies or the trustworthiness of a person or object*.

Ironically, even the word "of" in Matthew 4:1 has significance. It describes *an assault* and indicates that Jesus was assaulted by the devil. This took place at the end of the 40 days when Jesus was hungry, or "hungred," which in Greek is the word *peinao*, and it means *to be famished* and pictures *extreme hunger*. When Jesus was at His weakest point physically, mentally, and emotionally, the devil assaulted Him.

This all took place immediately after Jesus had been filled with the Holy Spirit and received the power of God. The Spirit led Him into a barren, isolated place where He was tempted and tested of the devil. God's purpose through it all was to show Jesus — and us — how great the baptism in the Holy Spirit is. Jesus was stronger than the devil as a result of being baptized in the Holy Spirit. The Spirit was working mightily within Him, empowering Him as human flesh with greater capacity to overcome the temptations and the methods of Satan to undermine and deceive or confuse. The same is true for us when we are baptized in the Holy Spirit.

Mark's Gospel Parallels Matthew in Many Ways

When we come to the gospel of Mark, we find a very similar recounting of Jesus' baptism and time of temptation in the wilderness. In Mark 1:7 and 8, John the Baptist told the people, "…There cometh one mightier than I after me, the latchet of whose shoes I am not worthy to stoop down and unloose. I indeed have baptized you with water: but he shall baptize you with the Holy Ghost."

Again, we see the word "baptize"— the Greek word *baptidzo* — which means *total immersion*. It described *the process of dipping a cloth or garment into a vat of color to dye it*. Historically, when it was finally removed from the dye, its appearance was totally different, and there was permanent resulting change. The Holy Spirit used this word a second time to indicate a full immersion in Him.

When you are baptized in the Holy Spirit, you soak up His power and His personality. This experience permanently changes you. It's not just a tiny touch; it is total transformation.

Mark 1:9 and 10 goes on to say, "And it came to pass in those days, that Jesus came from Nazareth of Galilee, and was baptized of John in Jordan. And straightway coming up out of the water, he saw the heavens opened, and the Spirit like a dove descending upon him."

Once more we see the word "like," which is the Greek word *husei*. It means *as*. When the Holy Spirit descended, He didn't physically come as a dove. He came with the same gentle nature of a dove and settled "upon" Jesus. The word "upon" is the Greek word *epi*, and it means the Spirit rested *on* Jesus.

Some Unique Aspects Mark Includes

Mark 1:12 and 13 says, "And immediately the Spirit driveth him into the wilderness. And he was there in the wilderness forty days, tempted of Satan; and was with the wild beasts…."

In Mark's account, we see that the Spirit "driveth" Jesus into the wilderness. The word "driveth" is the Greek word *ekballo*, and it means *to hurl; to throw out*. This means that verse 12 could literally be translated, "And the

Spirit *hurled* or *propelled* Him into the wilderness immediately — *without delay.*"

Again we see the word "wilderness," which in Greek is the same word we saw in Matthew's gospel — the word *eremia*. It describes *a remote, isolated location in the middle of nowhere. It was an obscure, unfrequented place off the beaten path that was encountered when one traveled by foot, and it often proved to be quite dangerous, as there was little or no water and sustenance.* This was where the Spirit of God led Jesus to be "tempted of Satan."

The word "tempted" is the Greek word *peiradzo*, which means *to put to the test; to test in order to expose the truth about the quality of a substance.* It pictures *a test designed to expose deficiencies or the trustworthiness of a person or object.* Satan knew that Jesus had just been baptized in the Holy Spirit, and he came to test Him to see if He could be broken. The word "Satan" is the Greek word *Satanas*, which describes *Satan or the devil; one who hates, accuses, slanders, or conspires against; the adversary.*

What Satan did to Jesus is the same thing he does to you. When you are empowered by the Holy Spirit and you're standing on God's Word, he comes to test you to see if you are going to trust God and hold on to Scripture, or if you will give up. The baptism in the Holy Spirit gave Jesus the power He needed to withstand the enemy — even in His weakened physical state. That same strength is available to you.

One other unique feature of Mark's account is that it says Jesus was in the wilderness with the "wild beasts." The words "wild beasts" is the Greek word *therion*, and it denotes *a wild beast; a dangerous animal.* It pictures *vicious killers.* Amazingly, Jesus wasn't defeated by a wild animal or the lack of food and water or the devil's temptations. He had the power of the Holy Spirit and was victorious over all these challenges.

Luke's Account Is Similar, With a Few Additional Details

The Holy Spirit also moved on the physician Luke to include the story of Jesus' baptism. Luke 3:21 and 22 says, "Now when all the people were baptized, it came to pass, that Jesus also being baptized, and praying, the heaven was opened. And the Holy Ghost descended in a bodily shape like a dove upon him...." These verses are very similar to Matthew 3:16 and Mark 1:9 and 10.

Likewise, Luke 3:16 mirrors Matthew 3:11 and Mark 1:7 and 8. It says, "John answered, saying unto them all, I indeed baptize you with water; but one mightier than I cometh, the latchet of whose shoes I am not worthy to unloose: he shall baptize you with the Holy Ghost and with fire." Clearly, it is very important for us to know that Jesus is the One who baptizes us in the Holy Spirit. Otherwise, the Lord would not have included this truth three separate times in Scripture.

When we come to Luke 4, we begin reading about Jesus' great temptation in the wilderness. It is here that Luke gives us a few insights that are different from the other gospels. He said, "And Jesus being full of the Holy Ghost returned from Jordan, and was led by the Spirit into the wilderness, being forty days tempted of the devil. And in those days he did eat nothing: and when they were ended, he afterward hungered" (vv. 1,2).

Notice the word "full" in this verse. It is the Greek word *pleres*, and it means *full; complete; lacking nothing*. When Jesus received the baptism in the Holy Spirit, He was *full, complete, and lacked nothing*. He had everything He needed for His ministry and for living victoriously on earth. His time of testing in the wilderness proved just how powerful the Holy Spirit was in His life.

This verse also says **Jesus was "led by the Spirit."** In Greek, this actually says *in the control of the Holy Spirit; in the sphere of the Spirit; being dominated by the Spirit*. The passage then includes the Greek words *eremia*, translated here as "wilderness," and *peiradzo*, translated here as "tempted," which we have previously examined.

For 40 days, **Jesus was "tempted of the devil."** Matthew, Mark, and Luke all include this in their accounts. The word "devil" is the Greek word *diabolos*, and it describes *the devil or characteristics of the devil; one who repetitiously strikes until successfully penetrating an object in order to ruin it, affect it, or take it captive*. When the devil came to tempt Jesus, he was trying to penetrate His mind, will, and emotions in order to ruin Him and take Him captive. But he was unsuccessful.

Jesus "did eat nothing." The word "nothing" here is the Greek word *ouden*, and it means *absolutely nothing; emphatically nothing*. After the 40 days were ended, the Scripture says Jesus "hungered." Here again we see the Greek word *peinao*, which means *extreme hunger; to be famished*. At the end of Jesus' fasting, He was physically weak. Yet He did not give in to Satan's temptations.

Luke 4:14 and 15 goes on to say, "And Jesus returned in the power of the Spirit into Galilee: and there went out a fame of him through all the region round about. And he taught in their synagogues, being glorified of all."

Jesus came out of that time of testing in *power*. The word "power" is the Greek word *dunamis*, and it describes *power; explosive, superhuman power that comes with enormous energy and produces phenomenal, extraordinary, and unparalleled results*. The word *dunamis* depicts *mighty deeds that are impressive, incomparable, and beyond human ability to perform; miraculous power or miraculous manifestations*. It also describes *the power of an advancing army*. This means that when Jesus returned to Galilee, God's power was marching forward through Him with the strength of a mighty army.

Like it empowered Jesus, the baptism in the Holy Spirit will empower *you* — even in your weakest moment — to resist temptation and overcome evil. If you have not received this gift from God, give us a call at 1-800-742-5593, and we will pray with you to be baptized in the Holy Spirit.

STUDY QUESTIONS

Study to shew thyself approved unto God, a workman that needeth not to be ashamed, rightly dividing the word of truth.
— 2 Timothy 2:15

1. Reread the meaning of the word "baptize" — the Greek word *baptidzo*. How does this definition expand your understanding of what it means to be baptized in the Holy Spirit?

2. After Jesus received the baptism in the Holy Spirit at the Jordan River, the Bible says He was "full" of the Spirit, which means He was *full, complete*, and *lacked nothing*. Although the same is true for us when we are baptized in the Spirit, why do we sometimes experience a sense of lack in our lives? What can you do to regain and maintain a sense of fullness? (*See* 1 Timothy 4:14; 2 Timothy 1:6; Jude 20.)

PRACTICAL APPLICATION

But be ye doers of the word, and not hearers only, deceiving your own selves.
— James 1:22

1. What has been your understanding of the baptism of the Holy Spirit prior to this lesson?
2. If you have been baptized in the Holy Spirit, you have tasted of the amazing power of God. What might you share from your experience with a friend who wants to ask God for the baptism in the Holy Spirit, but he or she is afraid?

TOPIC
Power To Minister to Others

SCRIPTURES

1. **Luke 3:16** — John answered, saying unto them all, I indeed baptize you with water; but one mightier than I cometh, the latchet of whose shoes I am not worthy to unloose: he shall baptize you with the Holy Ghost and with fire.

2. **Luke 3:21,22** — Now when all the people were baptized, it came to pass, that Jesus also being baptized, and praying, the heaven was opened. And the Holy Ghost descended in a bodily shape like a dove upon him....

3. **Luke 4:1,2** — And Jesus being full of the Holy Ghost returned from Jordan, and was led by the Spirit into the wilderness, being forty days tempted of the devil. And in those days he did eat nothing: and when they were ended, he afterward hungered.

4. **Luke 4:14-18** — And Jesus returned in the power of the Spirit into Galilee: and there went out a fame of him through all the region round about. And he taught in their synagogues, being glorified of all. And he came to Nazareth, where he had been brought up: and, as his custom was, he went into the synagogue on the sabbath day, and stood up for to read. And there was delivered unto him the book of the prophet Esaias. And when he had opened the book, he found the place where it was written. The Spirit of the Lord is upon me, because he hath anointed me to preach the gospel to the poor; he hath sent me to heal the brokenhearted, to preach deliverance to the captives,

and recovering of sight to the blind, to set at liberty them that are bruised. To preach the acceptable year of the Lord.

GREEK WORDS

1. "baptize" — βαπτίζω (*baptidzo*): a word that originally meant to dip and dye; in early usage, it described the process of dipping a cloth or garment into a vat of color to dye it, leaving it there long enough for the material to soak up the new color, and then pulling that garment out of the dye with a permanently changed outward appearance; to baptize; to fully immerse

2. "like" — ὡσεὶ (*husei*): not *just like*, but *as*

3. "upon" — ἐπί (*epi*): upon; on

4. "full" — πλήρης (*pleres*): full; complete; lacking nothing

5. "by" — ἐν (*en*): in the control of; in the sphere of

6. "wilderness" — ἐρημία (*eremia*): a remote, isolated location in the middle of nowhere; a remote place that is out of the way; somewhere off the beaten track; an obscure site or an unfrequented location; such places were often encountered when one traveled by foot, and they often proved to be dangerous because there was little water and no sustenance

7. "tempted" — πειράζω (*peiradzo*): to put to the test; to test in order to prove; to test in order to expose the truth about the quality of a substance; pictures a test designed to expose deficiencies or the trustworthiness of a person or object

8. "devil" — διάβολος (*diabolos*): devil; characteristic of the devil, one who repetitiously strikes until successfully penetrating an object in order to ruin it, affect it, or take it captive

9. "nothing" — οὐδὲν (*ouden*): absolutely nothing; emphatically nothing

10. "hungred" — πεινάω (*peinao*): pictures extreme hunger; to be famished

11. "power" — δύναμις (*dunamis*): power; explosive, superhuman power that comes with enormous energy and produces phenomenal, extraordinary, and unparalleled results; depicts "mighty deeds" that are impressive, incomparable, and beyond human ability to perform; miraculous power or miraculous manifestations

12. "because" — ἕνεκεν (*heneka*): because; on account of; indicates purpose

13. "anointed" — χρίω (*chrio*): originally denoted the smearing or rubbing of oil, medicine, or perfume upon an individual; used in a medical sense to denote healing ointment; scripturally used to denote the anointing of the Holy Spirit and all the effects that the anointing imparts

14. "to preach the gospel" — εὐαγγελίσασθαί (*euangelisasthai*): to announce good news; to preach good news; to channel good news

15. "poor" — πτωχός (*ptochos*): pertaining to abject poverty; impoverished

16. "brokenhearted" — συντρίβω (*suntribo*): used to describe the crushing of grapes with the feet, or the smashing and grinding of bones into dust; depicts people who have been walked on by others, those who have been crushed by others, or those who feel they have been smashed to pieces by life or relationships

17. "heal" — ἰάομαι (*iaomai*): to cure; usually refers to a progressive cure; often depicts a healing power that progressively reverses a condition over a period of time, or a sickness that is progressively healed rather than instantaneously healed

18. "preach" — κηρύσσω (*kerusso*): to preach, proclaim, declare, announce, or herald a message

19. "deliverance" — ἄφεσις (*aphesis*): a release; a dismissal; a pardon; to set free; to loose

20. "captives" — αἰχμάλωτος (*aichmalotos*): prisoners; captives; those taken captive at the point of a spear; those who are dragged into bondage

21. "recovering of sight" — ἀνάβλεψις *(anablepsis)*: the returning of one's sight; the restoration of sight; to see again

22. "blind" — τυφλός (*tuphlos*): blind; it doesn't just depict a person who is unable to see, but a person who has been intentionally blinded by someone else; can picture one whose eyes have been deliberately removed so that he is blinded; that individual hasn't just lost his sight, he has no eyes with which to see

23. "set at liberty" — ἄφεσις (*aphesis*): a release; a dismissal; a pardon; to loose; to set free, in this case, from the detrimental effects of a shattered life; the Greek speaks of a release from the destructive effects of brokenness

24. "bruised" — τεθραυσμένους (*tethrausmenous*): to crush; to break down; depicts a person who has been shattered or fractured by life;

pictures those whose lives have been continually split up and fragmented

25. "acceptable" — δεκτό (*dektos*): favorable; accepted; a favorable time to
receive

SYNOPSIS

When Jesus was water-baptized in the Jordan River, He was also baptized
in the Holy Spirit. John the Baptist testified that God did not "...give
Him [Jesus] His Spirit sparingly or by measure, but boundless is the gift
God makes of His Spirit (John 3:34 *AMPC*). Immediately after this, Jesus
was led by the Spirit into the wilderness to be tempted of the devil (*see*
Luke 4:10). It was in the Judean wilderness, not far from the Jordan River,
that Jesus defeated Satan with the power of the Holy Spirit and the Word
of God. He then returned to the region of Galilee in the power of the
Spirit to minister to others.

The emphasis of this lesson:

**When you receive the baptism in the Holy Spirit, you are supernatu-
rally empowered to minister to others. God's empowerment is meant to
flow through you to transform people's lives.**

John Baptized Jesus in the Jordan

In our last lesson, we learned about John the Baptist — the man sent by
God to prepare the way for Jesus' arrival. When the people asked John
if he was the Messiah, "John answered, saying unto them all, I indeed
baptize you with water; but one mightier than I cometh, the latchet of
whose shoes I am not worthy to unloose: he shall baptize you with the
Holy Ghost and with fire" (Luke 3:16).

Twice in this verse, the word "baptize" appears, which is the Greek word
baptidzo, meaning *to fully immerse*. Originally, this word meant *to dip and
dye*. In its early usage, it described *the process of dipping a cloth or garment
into a vat of color to dye it, leaving it there long enough for the material to soak
up the new color, and then pulling that garment out of the dye with a permanently changed outward appearance.*

The baptism John offered was one of confession of sin and repentance.
And just as he was fully immersing people in the waters of the Jordan
River, he said there was One coming after him who would fully immerse

people in the Holy Spirit and fire. This Baptizer was Jesus, and when He came He would saturate individuals in the Holy Spirit so powerfully that they would be permanently transformed.

But before Jesus became the Baptizer, He Himself was baptized. Luke 3:21 and 22 says, "Now when all the people were baptized, it came to pass, that Jesus also being baptized, and praying, the heaven was opened. And the Holy Ghost descended in a bodily shape like a dove upon him…."

We saw that the word "like" is the Greek word *husei*, which means *not just like, but as*. When the Holy Spirit descended on Jesus, He did not come in the form of a physical bird. He came *as* a dove, which means *He acted as a dove — He came with a gentle nature and rested upon Jesus*. With the Holy Spirit resting and remaining on Jesus gently, He was powerfully able to resist the temptations of the enemy and remain faithful to God.

Jesus Was Full of the Holy Spirit

Luke 4 opens, saying, "And Jesus being *full* of the Holy Ghost returned from Jordan, and was led by the Spirit into the wilderness, being forty days tempted of the devil. And in those days he did eat nothing: and when they were ended, he afterward hungered" (Luke 4:1,2).

We learned that the word "full" in verse 1 is the Greek word *pleres*, which means *full; complete; lacking nothing*. That is what Jesus received when He was baptized in the Holy Spirit — the full, complete empowerment of God's Spirit. In fact, He was so filled with the Spirit that He *lacked nothing*. The same holds true for you when you are baptized in the Holy Spirit. You are given everything you need to live a holy, victorious life — you lack nothing.

Interestingly, Jesus discovered just how full of the Spirit He was when the devil came to test Him. The Bible says He was "tempted of the devil" for 40 days. The Greek word for "tempted" is *peiradzo*, which means *to put to the test; to test in order to expose the truth about the quality of a substance*. It pictures *a test designed to expose deficiencies or the trustworthiness of a person or object*.

Satan tempted Jesus to see what He was made of. Would He live up to His divine reputation, or would He yield to temptation? The enemy got his answer as Jesus stood unflinchingly and spoke the Word against him.

Even in a weak, depleted physical condition, Jesus had all the power He needed to defeat the devil and not give in to His human nature.

Luke 4:15 says, "And Jesus returned in the power of the Spirit into Galilee: and there went out a fame of him through all the region round about." The word "power" here is the old Greek word *dunamis*, which describes *explosive, superhuman power that comes with enormous energy and produces phenomenal, extraordinary, and unparalleled results*. It also depicts *the full might of an advancing army*. When the Roman army advanced, *dunamis* was the word used to describe them. They had the power to conquer anything that stood in their way. That is the kind of power that was released through Jesus when He returned from the wilderness to Galilee.

What Did the Baptism of the Holy Spirit Mean in Jesus' Life?

The Bible says, "And he [Jesus] came to Nazareth, where he had been brought up: and, as his custom was, he went into the synagogue on the sabbath day, and stood up for to read. And there was delivered unto him the book of the prophet Esaias. And when he had opened the book, he found the place where it was written. The Spirit of the Lord is upon me, because he hath anointed me to preach the gospel to the poor; he hath sent me to heal the brokenhearted, to preach deliverance to the captives, and recovering of sight to the blind, to set at liberty them that are bruised. To preach the acceptable year of the Lord" (Luke 4:16-18).

The Spirit was "upon" Jesus. The word "upon" is the Greek *epi*, which means *upon or on*. When Jesus said the Spirit was "upon" Him, He was referring back to the moment when He was baptized in the Holy Spirit at the Jordan River. From then on, the Spirit of God rested upon Him.

Jesus was "anointed." The word "anointed" in verse 18 is the Greek word *chrio*, which *originally denoted the smearing or rubbing of oil, medicine, or perfume upon an individual*. The word was used in a medical sense to denote *healing ointment*. Scripturally, it was used to denote *the anointing of the Holy Spirit and all the effects that the anointing imparts*.

It's interesting to note that in those days, when someone was anointed, it was done through a person's hands. The healing oil or medicine was placed on the anointer's hands and then rubbed onto the one being anointed. Thus, if you were being anointed, you were receiving *a hands-on experience*.

When Jesus said, "The Spirit of the Lord is upon me because he hath anointed me," He was saying, "God's hand is on Me. He has placed His hands on My life and His healing power has been worked into Me."

In other words, Jesus was anointed:

- **"To preach the Gospel."** This phrase is the Greek word *euangelisasthai*, and it means *to announce good news; to preach good news; to channel good news*. The very earliest known use of this word was to describe *a medium or a person who channeled evil spirits*. In this Scripture passage, however, it is used in a godly way. Essentially, Jesus said, "God has anointed Me to be *an open channel or conduit* for the Good News to reach the *poor*." The word "poor" is also important. It is the Greek word *ptochos*, and it describes *abject poverty*, or *those who are impoverished*. Jesus was anointed by God to bring economic changes to those living in destitution.

- **"To heal the brokenhearted."** The word "brokenhearted" is the Greek word *suntribo*, and it was used to describe *the crushing of grapes with the feet*, or *the smashing and grinding of bones into dust*. Taken in context, this word depicts *people who have been walked on by others, those who have been crushed by others, or those who feel they have been smashed to pieces by life or relationships*.

  By using the word *suntribo* — translated here as "brokenhearted" — Jesus was saying, "For those who have been crushed by others and feel walked on or smashed to pieces by life and relationships, I am anointed to heal." The word "heal" in this verse is the Greek word *iaomai*, which means *to cure*, and it usually refers to *a progressive cure*. This word often depicts *a healing power that progressively reverses a condition over a period of time, or a sickness that is progressively healed rather than instantaneously healed*.

- **"To preach deliverance to the captives."** Three words are important in this phrase. First is the word "preach," which is the Greek word *kerusso*, meaning to *preach, proclaim, declare, announce, or herald a message*. Second is the word "deliverance," which in Greek is the word *aphesis*, which describes *a release; a dismissal; a pardon*. It can also mean *to set free; to loose*.

  The word "captives" is also significant. It is the Greek word describing *prisoners or captives; those taken captive at the point of a spear*. These are people *who have been dragged into bondage by force against their will*. This captivity can be to any number of things, including a poor self-image, damaging relationships, bad habits, drugs, or any type of addiction. Jesus said He came to proclaim and declare release and freedom to all those held captive.

- **"And recovering of sight to the blind."** The phrase "recovering of sight" is the Greek word *anablepsis*, which means *the returning of one's sight; the restoration of sight; to see again.* And the word "blind" is the Greek word *tuphlos*, which doesn't just depict a person who is unable to see, but *a person who has been intentionally blinded by someone else.* The word *tuphlos* can picture *one whose eyes have been deliberately removed so that he is blinded.* The individual *hasn't just lost his sight — he has no eyes with which to see.*

As a result of great difficulties and challenging situations, people can become "blind" to reality and the power of God. Jesus declared that He was anointed by God to restore the sight of those who have been intentionally blinded by the enemy. He even has the power to give people eyes to see again.

- **"To set at liberty them that are bruised."** The phrase "set at liberty" is again the Greek word *aphesis* — the same word translated as "deliverance" earlier in the verse. It describes *a release, a dismissal,* or *a pardon.* It means *to loose* or *to set free,* and in this case, *to set free from the detrimental effects of a shattered life.* Here the Greek speaks of a release from the destructive effects of brokenness.

This brings us to the word "bruised," which is the Greek word that means *to crush* or *to break down.* It depicts *a person who has been shattered or fractured by life.* It denotes *those whose lives have been continually split up and fragmented.* Jesus declared that He had been baptized in the Holy Spirit and received power to release people from this kind of broken existence.

- **"To preach the acceptable year of the Lord."** The word "acceptable" is the Greek word *dektos,* and it means *favorable; accepted; a favorable time to receive.* What this means is that when Jesus' anointing shows up, it is the most favorable moment in a person's life to receive the supernatural help and healing that is needed.

All these amazing blessings were available to people through Jesus as a result of His being baptized in the Holy Spirit! When you receive the baptism in the Holy Spirit, you have the same anointing on your life to do extraordinary things. The Spirit empowers you to be a channel to preach the

Gospel to the poor. His power comes in you to flow through you to others, including the sick, the fearful, the depressed, and those broken by life.

STUDY QUESTIONS

Study to shew thyself approved unto God, a workman that
needeth not to be ashamed, rightly dividing the word of truth.
— 2 Timothy 2:15

1. When you are baptized in the Holy Spirit, you are *full, complete,* and *lack nothing.* Meditate on the message of First Peter 1:3 and Ephesians 1:3. What is the Holy Spirit showing you in these verses about what He has made available to you every day of your journey?
2. Carefully read the powerful truths in Second Timothy 3:16 and Second Peter 1:20 and 21. What is the connection between the Word of God (Scripture) and the Holy Spirit?
3. Why is it vital that you understand this connection in light of your *personal spiritual growth?* Why is it vital in order to help you effectively minister to others? (Consider John 14:26; 16:13,14; Luke 12:11,12.)

PRACTICAL APPLICATION

But be ye doers of the word, and not hearers only,
deceiving your own selves.
— James 1:22

1. As a believer, you represent Christ on the earth at this time in history. Take these words He spoke in Luke 4:16-18 and *speak them out loud* as a personal declaration: "The Spirit of the Lord is upon *me*, because [God] hath anointed *me* to preach the gospel to the poor; he hath sent *me* to heal the brokenhearted, to preach deliverance to the captives, and recovering of sight to the blind, to set at liberty them that are bruised. To preach the acceptable year of the Lord."
2. What does declaring this powerful passage over your life stir up inside of you?
3. As a child of God, you are anointed to be a blessing to others everywhere you go. Look back over your life. Where and in what specific ways can you see the hand of the Lord on your life? How has His anointing on you impacted the lives of others?

TOPIC

Power for Every Believer

SCRIPTURES

1. **John 20:21,22** — Then said Jesus to them again, Peace be unto you: as my Father hath sent me, even so send I you. And when he had said this, he breathed on them, and saith unto them, Receive ye the Holy Ghost.

2. **Luke 24:49** — And, behold, I send the promise of my Father upon you: but tarry ye in the city of Jerusalem, until ye be endued with power from on high.

3. **Acts 1:4,5** — And, being assembled together with them, commanded them that they should not depart from Jerusalem, but wait for the promise of the Father, which, saith he, ye have heard of me. For John truly baptized with water; but ye shall be baptized with the Holy Ghost not many days hence.

4. **Acts 1:8** — But ye shall receive power, after that the Holy Ghost is come upon you: and ye shall be witnesses unto me both in Jerusalem, and in all Judaea, and in Samaria, and unto the uttermost part of the earth.

5. **Acts 2:1-4** — And when the day of Pentecost was fully come, they were all with one accord in one place. And suddenly there came a sound from heaven as a rushing mighty wind, and it filled all the house where they were sitting. And there appeared unto them cloven tongues like as of fire, and it sat upon each of them. And they were all filled with the Holy Ghost, and began to speak with other tongues, as the Spirit gave them utterance.

6. **Acts 8:12** — When they believed Philip preaching the things concerning the kingdom of God, and the name of Jesus Christ, they were baptized, both men and women.

7. **Acts 8:14,15** — Now when the apostles which were at Jerusalem heard that Samaria had received the word of God, they sent unto them Peter and John Who, when they were come down, prayed for them, that they might receive the Holy Ghost.

8. **Romans 8:9** — ...now if any man have not the Spirit of Christ, he is none of his.

9. **Acts 8:16-21** — For as yet he was fallen upon none of them... Then laid they their hands on them, and they received the Holy Ghost. And when Simon saw that through laying on of the apostles' hands the Holy Ghost was given, he offered them money, saying, Give me also this power, that on whomsoever I lay hands, he may receive the Holy Ghost. But Peter said unto him, Thy money perish with thee, because thou hast thought that the gift of God may be purchased with money. Thou hast neither part nor lot in this matter: for thy heart is not right in the sight of God.

10. **Acts 9:17** — And Ananias went his way, and entered into the house; and putting his hands on him said, Brother Saul, the Lord, even Jesus, that appeared unto thee in the way as thou camest, hath sent me, that thou mightest receive thy sight, and be filled with the Holy Ghost.

11. **1 Corinthians 14:18** — I thank my God, I speak with tongues more than ye all.

12. **Acts 10:44** — While Peter yet spake these words, the Holy Ghost fell on all them which heard the word.

13. **Acts 10:46** — For they heard them speak with tongues, and magnify God....

14. **Acts 19:3-6** — And he said unto them, Unto what then were ye baptized? And they said, Unto John's baptism. Then, said Paul, John verily baptized with the baptism of repentance, saying unto the people, that they should believe on him which should come after him, that is, on Christ Jesus. When they heard this, they were baptized in the name of the Lord Jesus. And when Paul had laid his hands upon them, the Holy Ghost came on them; and they spake with tongues, and prophesied.

GREEK WORDS

1. "breathed on them"— ἐμφυσάω (*emphusao*): to breathe into; to inflate; it is the same word used in Genesis 2:7

2. "upon"— ἐπί (*epi*): upon; on

3. "endued"— ἐνδύω (*enduo*): the act of putting on a garment or a piece of clothing; presents the idea of sinking into a garment and becoming at ease in it; the usage of this word means certain traits will be

operative only when they are deliberately picked up, put on by choice, as one would dress himself in a new set of clothes

4. "power" — δύναμις (*dunamis*): power; explosive, superhuman power that comes with enormous energy and produces phenomenal, extraordinary, and unparalleled results; depicts "mighty deeds" that are impressive, incomparable, and beyond human ability to perform; miraculous power or miraculous manifestations

5. "shall receive" — λαμβάνω (*lambano*): to seize or to lay hold of something in order to make it your very own, almost like a person who reaches out to grab, to capture, or to take possession of something; at other times, it depicts one who graciously receives something that is freely and easily given

6. "filled" — πλήθω (*pletho*): filled to capacity

7. "power" — ἐξουσία (*exousia*): delegated authority; influence; denotes one who has delegated power; often translated as "authority"

8. "matter" — λόγος (*logos*): a word in this speaking; a word in this form of verbal communication

9. "filled" — πλήθω (*pletho*): to fill to capacity

10. "I speak" — λαλῶ (*lalo*): I converse, I speak fluently; I speak conversationally

11. "more than" — μᾶλλον (*mallon*): comparatively more; more than compared to what others do

12. "ye all" — πάντων ὑμῶν (*panton humon*): all; all of you combined

13. "fell on" — ἐπιπίπτω (*epipipto*): to fall upon; to rush upon

SYNOPSIS

When John the Baptist spoke on the banks of the Jordan River about Jesus, he gave people a preview of who Jesus was and why He was coming into the world. In three of the four gospels, it is recorded that he focused on the fact that Jesus would be the One to baptize people in the Holy Spirit. This declaration from John's lips was straight from God's heart. Jesus' intention from the very beginning was not only to save people from their sins, but also to immerse them in His Holy Spirit. The baptism in the Holy Spirit is meant to empower every believer, not just a select few.

The emphasis of this lesson:

The baptism in the Holy Spirit was not just for the leaders of the Early Church and those in ministry today. It's for every believer. There is a distinct pattern throughout the book of Acts that confirms this.

The day Jesus rose from the grave, He appeared to His disciples. The Bible says, "Then said Jesus to them again, Peace be unto you: as my Father hath sent me, even so send I you. And when he had said this, he breathed on them, and saith unto them, Receive ye the Holy Ghost" (John 20:21,22).

The phrase "breathed on them" is the Greek word *emphusao*, which means *to breathe into; to inflate*. It is the same word used in Genesis 2:7 to describe *when God breathed into Adam's nostrils the breath of life*. The moment Jesus breathed into His disciples is the moment they were born again. The Holy Spirit of God came into each of them at that precise moment.

Before that time, they had experienced the presence of the Holy Spirit; He had come *upon* them for times of ministry to others. However, it wasn't until Jesus had been resurrected and then *breathed* on them (John 20:22) that the Holy Spirit actually came to live *inside* of them and they were born again.

The Baptism in the Holy Spirit Provides Powerful Spiritual Clothing

Just before Jesus was taken up into Heaven, He gathered His devoted followers and told them, "Behold, I send the promise of my Father upon you: but tarry ye in the city of Jerusalem, until ye be endued with power from on high" (Luke 24:49). The word "Behold" is one of great exclamation. It was the equivalent of Jesus saying, "Wow! What I'm about to tell you is so amazing it nearly leaves me speechless."

He then said, "I send the promise of My Father upon you...." The word "upon" here is the Greek word *epi*, which means *on*. Remember, the Holy Spirit had already come *into* them when Jesus breathed on them. That is when they were saved. So this experience Jesus was describing is secondary to the salvation experience — it is the baptism in the Holy Spirit.

The disciples were told to wait in Jerusalem until they were "endued with power from on high." The word "endued" is the Greek word *enduo*, and it denotes *the act of putting on a garment or a piece of clothing*. It presents the idea of *sinking into a garment and becoming at ease in it*. The usage of this word means certain traits will be operative only when they are deliberately picked up and put on by choice, as one would dress himself in a new set of clothes.

From this word *enduo*, we see that it was God's intention that the disciples would receive the Spirit's power and sink into it like a comfortable set of clothes. He wanted them to take by faith the power He was sending and to choose to put it on in the same way they would put on a new set of clothes each morning.

Jesus called this new clothing "power," which is the Greek word *dunamis*. It describes *power; explosive, superhuman power that comes with enormous energy and produces phenomenal, extraordinary, and unparalleled results*. It depicts *"mighty deeds" that are impressive, incomparable, and beyond human ability to perform; miraculous power or miraculous manifestations*. This is the baptism in the Holy Spirit — a new set of clothes that provide the wearer with amazing, supernatural power.

Jesus' Instructions To Wait for the Power

In Acts 1:4 and 5, it says, "And, being assembled together with them, commanded them that they should not depart from Jerusalem, but wait for the promise of the Father, which, saith he, ye have heard of me. For John truly baptized with water; but ye shall be baptized with the Holy Ghost not many days hence."

Here again, we see the word "baptize" in verse 5. This is the Greek word *baptidzo*, which means *to be fully immersed* in the Holy Spirit. And this would take place "not many days hence." In other words, this experience was a future one — one that had not happened yet. It was secondary to salvation.

In Acts 1:8, Jesus went on to say, "But ye shall receive power, after that the Holy Ghost is come upon you: and ye shall be witnesses unto me both in Jerusalem, and in all Judaea, and in Samaria, and unto the uttermost part of the earth." The phrase "shall receive" is the Greek word *lambano*, which means *to seize or to lay hold of something in order to make it your very own, almost like a person who reaches out to grab, to capture, or to take possession of something*. At other times, it depicts *one who graciously receives something that is freely and easily given*.

The word "power" in verse 8 is *dunamis* — the same Greek word we saw in Luke 24:49. It depicts explosive, superhuman power that yields extraordinary results. Jesus said this power would come "upon" them. The word "upon" is again the Greek word *epi*, meaning *on* or *upon*. By using this word, Jesus described a distinct experience that is subsequent to salvation. When the disciples were born again, the Holy Spirit came to live inside them; the baptism of the Holy Spirit was Him coming *upon* them.

There Is a Distinct Pattern for Receiving the Baptism in the Holy Spirit

In addition to being a history book of the First Century Church, the book of Acts is also a *pattern book* for believers in all generations. When you study Acts, you will see there is pattern of how God works in individuals' lives as well as within His Church corporately, and it all began on the Day of Pentecost.

Acts 2:1-4. "And when the day of Pentecost was fully come, they were all with one accord in one place. And suddenly there came a sound from heaven as a rushing mighty wind, and it filled all the house where they were sitting. And there appeared unto them cloven tongues like as of fire, and it sat upon each of them. And they were all filled with the Holy Ghost, and began to speak with other tongues, as the Spirit gave them utterance."

The word "filled" in verse 2 is the Greek word *pletho*, which means *filled to capacity*. This tells us that what the people experienced in the Upper Room on the Day of Pentecost was not just a "little touch" of God's Spirit. On the contrary, they were filled to capacity with the Holy Spirit, and there was such an overflow that it began to pour forth out of their mouths. Literally, they began to speak in other tongues as the Spirit gave them utterance.

Acts 8 — One Year After Pentecost. The events recorded in this chapter reveal a distinct pattern. Verse 12 says, "When they believed Philip preaching the things concerning the kingdom of God, and the name of Jesus Christ, they were baptized, both men and women." After Philip preached the Good News in Samaria, many people believed on Jesus — they were born again. They were then baptized in water.

Acts 8:14-16 tells us, "Now when the apostles which were at Jerusalem heard that Samaria had received the word of God, they sent unto them Peter and John Who, when they were come down, prayed for them, that they might receive the Holy Ghost. (For as yet he was fallen upon none of them: only they were baptized in the name of the Lord Jesus.)"

Here we see a clear pattern: the Gospel was preached; the people believed and accepted Christ; and they were baptized in water. But they had not yet received the baptism in the Holy Spirit. That was the reason Peter and John went down to meet with them — to pray that they would be clothed with the power of the Spirit. Verse 17 says, "Then laid they their hands on them, and they received the Holy Ghost."

Although it doesn't explicitly say that the Samaritans spoke in tongues, we know they did from the subsequent verses. Acts 8:18-20 says, "And when Simon saw that through laying on of the apostles' hands the Holy Ghost was given, he offered them money, saying, Give me also this power, that on whomsoever I lay hands, he may receive the Holy Ghost. But Peter said unto him, Thy money perish with thee, because thou hast thought that the gift of God may be purchased with money. Thou hast neither part nor lot in this matter: for thy heart is not right in the sight of God."

According to verse 18, Simon saw something that clearly confirmed that the Samaritans had been baptized in the Holy Spirit. This former sorcerer was familiar with and drawn to the supernatural, so when he saw the evidence of the Holy Spirit's baptism, he asked Peter and John to give him the same "power." The word "power" here is the Greek word *exousia*, which actually means *delegated* authority; *influence*.

Immediately, the disciples rejected Simon's offer to pay for the authority to pray for people to be baptized in the Holy Spirit. They said, "Thou hast neither part nor lot in this matter…" (vs. 21). The word "matter" in this verse is the word *logos*, which is the Greek word for *verbal communication*. Thus, this verse could be translated, "Thou hast neither part nor lot in *this form of speaking or verbal communication*." What Simon "saw" when the disciples prayed for the Samaritans was them speaking in other tongues!

Acts 9 — Four Years After Pentecost. Saul was persecuting the Church, and he had just received permission from the Jewish leaders to expand his "search-and-destroy" mission to the believers in the city of Damascus. However, while he was on His way, Jesus met him on the road and stopped him in his tracks. Blinded by the light of Christ's glory, Saul was knocked to the ground and confessed that Jesus was Lord. In that moment, he was saved. He was then led by the hand into the city where he awaited further instruction from the Lord.

Meanwhile, the Holy Spirit began speaking to a believer by the name of Ananias, telling him about Saul's conversion on the Damascus Road and prompting him to go and pray for Saul to receive his sight and be baptized in the Holy Spirit. Acts 9:17 says, "And Ananias went his way, and entered into the house; and putting his hands on him said, Brother Saul, the Lord, even Jesus, that appeared unto thee in the way as thou camest, hath sent me, that thou mightest receive thy sight, and be filled with the Holy Ghost."

Immediately, Saul's eyes were opened and he was baptized in the Holy Spirit (*see* Acts 9:18). The word "filled" in verse 17 is the Greek word *pletho*, which means *to fill to capacity*. It is the same word used in Acts 2:4 describing the believers who were filled with the Holy Spirit on the Day of Pentecost. Although Acts 9 doesn't explicitly say Saul spoke in tongues, we know that he did from his own testimony in First Corinthians 14:18 when he told the believers, "I thank my God, I speak with tongues more than ye all."

Interestingly, the words "I speak" is the Greek word *lalo*, which means *I converse; I speak fluently; I speak conversationally*. This tells us that tongues was a real language to him that he spoke in fluently. In fact, Paul said he spoke in tongues "more than ye all." The words "more than" is the Greek word *mallon*, which means *comparatively more*, and "ye all" means *all of you combined*. This phrase was the equivalent of Paul saying, "Compared to everyone else, I speak in tongues more than all of you combined."

Acts 10: Seven Years After Pentecost. Clearly directed by the Holy Spirit, Peter was sought out and escorted to the house of a man named Cornelius. He was a Gentile who lived in the city of Caesarea and was deeply devoted to God. With great anticipation of what God would do, Cornelius gathered his entire family together to hear what Peter was going to share.

Acts 10:44 says, "While Peter yet spake these words, the Holy Ghost fell on all them which hear the word." While Peter was sharing the Good News about Jesus, the Holy Spirit "fell on" all the Gentiles. The words "fell on" is the Greek word *epipipto*, which means *to fall upon; to rush upon*. Verse

46 confirms that they were baptized in the Holy Spirit, saying, "For they heard them speak with tongues, and magnify God...."

Acts 19: Twenty-Three Years After Pentecost. In Acts 19, we find the apostle Paul returning to Ephesus, and when he arrived in the upper part of the city, he encountered a group of people who had been baptized by John the Baptist before Christ's appearing and who were still waiting for the Messiah to come.

Acts 19:3-5 says, "And he [Paul] said unto them, Unto what then were ye baptized? And they said, Unto John's baptism. Then, said Paul, John verily baptized with the baptism of repentance, saying unto the people, that they should believe on him which should come after him, that is, on Christ Jesus. When they heard this, they were baptized in the name of the Lord Jesus."

Once the people heard and understood that Jesus was the Messiah and that He had indeed come as John had predicted, they put their faith in Christ and were baptized in Christ's name. Verse 6 goes on to say, "When Paul had laid his hands upon them, the Holy Ghost came on them; and they spake with tongues, and prophesied." Once more, we see that the Spirit "came on" them — the Greek word *epi*, meaning *on*. This describes the secondary experience of the baptism in the Holy Spirit.

From the beginning of the book of Acts to the end, we see the same pattern repeated. People get saved and are baptized in water. They experience the baptism in the Holy Spirit, in which the Spirit comes *upon* them. Their hearts become so full of the Spirit that their mouths begin to speak the language of the Spirit, which is often called tongues.

STUDY QUESTIONS
**Study to shew thyself approved unto God, a workman that needeth not to be ashamed, rightly dividing the word of truth.
— 2 Timothy 2:15**

1. As a believer, you have been empowered by God to help others know Him. Read Second Corinthians 5:17-20 and describe every believer's overall calling.

2. Second Corinthians 12:4-11 reveals nine specific gifts the Holy Spirit distributes to God's people. Name these gifts and tell which one(s) the Lord has manifested through you.

3. The apostle Paul compares the Church and all its members to a physical body in Second Corinthians 12:12-26. Carefully read this passage and share how it helps you appreciate the gifts of others.

PRACTICAL APPLICATION

But be ye doers of the word, and not hearers only,
deceiving your own selves.
—James 1:22

1. Of all the accounts presented from the book of Acts, which inspires you most? Why?

2. The Lord wants you to be *comfortable* and *at ease* within the power of His Spirit. With what aspects of the baptism of the Holy Spirit are you most comfortable? What aspects make you uncomfortable? Pause and pray, "Lord, why do these things make me feel uneasy?"

3. Who do you know that desperately needs the baptism in the Spirit — they need the supernatural power of God in their lives to resist temptation, to experience God's healing or other blessing, or to experience the empowerment of the Spirit for life, ministry, *and victory*?

LESSON 4

TOPIC
Power To Move You
Into the Supernatural

SYNOPSIS

A life-changing event took place for Jesus at the Jordan River. Matthew 3:16 and 17 declares, "And Jesus, when he was baptized, went up straightway out of the water: and, lo, the heavens were opened unto him, and he saw the Spirit of God descending like a dove, and lighting upon him: and lo a voice from heaven, saying, This is my beloved Son, in whom I am well pleased."

At that precise moment, Jesus was not just water-baptized — He was baptized in the Holy Spirit and launched into ministry. In doing so, He established a pattern that all of us should follow. Since Jesus, the Son of God, needed the empowerment in the Holy Spirit, we certainly need His empowerment in *our* lives.

The emphasis of this lesson:

The baptism in the Holy Spirit is the power to move you into the supernatural.

The Baptism in the Holy Spirit Is Essential, Not Optional

Just before Jesus ascended into Heaven, He spoke a strong word of instruction to His devoted followers, which is recorded in Acts 1:4 and 5: "And, being assembled together with them, commanded them that they should not depart from Jerusalem, but wait for the promise of the Father, which, saith he, ye have heard of me. For John truly baptized with water; but ye shall be baptized with the Holy Ghost not many days hence."

From this passage, we see that Jesus "commanded" His disciples to wait for the Holy Spirit. In other words, receiving the baptism of the Holy Spirit was not optional — it was *essential*. We saw in our last lesson that by this time, the disciples were already saved. Jesus had "breathed on" them the day He was raised from the dead. He breathed into them the breath of His eternal nature and life, and they received the Holy Spirit and became born again (*see* John 20:19-22). Christ by His Spirit was living inside them.

Peace Plus Power

But there was a subsequent experience that God had designed for them to receive after their new birth, and the same is true for us. *Peace* comes to us the moment we are saved, but *power* comes to us when we receive the baptism in the Holy Spirit. This supernatural infilling is a secondary, subsequent experience that God intends for every believer to have.

To be clear, you do *not* have to speak in tongues to be saved and go to Heaven! And if you don't speak in tongues, you are not a second-class Christian. We are all saved the same way — by God's grace and through faith in the finished work of Jesus Christ. If you're born again, you have been washed by the blood of Jesus, your sins are forgiven, and you are on your way to Heaven. But the baptism in the Holy Spirit will give you the power you need to live an overcoming life on earth.

Where the Spirit of the Lord Is, There Is Freedom

People who have been baptized in the Holy Spirit are usually quite different from believers who don't believe in and have not been baptized in the Spirit. Likewise, churches that are often called "Spirit-filled" are usually quite different than mainline denominational churches who don't embrace the baptism in the Holy Spirit.

Churches and individuals who are Spirit-filled usually exude more love, joy, peace, patience, kindness, goodness, gentleness, faithfulness, and self-control. Churches and people who don't believe in the baptism in the Holy Spirit can sometimes be judgmental, legalistic, fearful, worldly, anxious, and unloving. They can be more like the world than like the Lord.

One of the greatest differences between a person who has been baptized in the Holy Spirit and one who has not is the level of *freedom* in which they walk. Second Corinthians 3:17 confirms this, declaring, "The Lord is that Spirit: and where the Spirit of the Lord is, there is liberty."

God's Intentions Are the Same Today as in the Early Church

Praying in tongues gives us the ability to speak to God in a supernatural language on the highest spiritual level possible. As we do, divine power is released in and through our lives. The Holy Spirit gives you power to resist evil and minister to the needs of others.

Realize that it is God's intention not just to save you and give you peace. He also wants to baptize you in His Holy Spirit, clothing you with power from on High. What He did in the lives of the early believers in the book of Acts, He desires to do in your life today. Those who were saved then were also subsequently baptized in the Holy Spirit and spoke with other tongues.

It all began on the Day of Pentecost. After 10 days of prayer in the Upper Room, the gift of the Holy Spirit descended on the Church like a rushing mighty wind. "And they were all filled with the Holy Ghost, and began to speak with other tongues, as the Spirit gave them utterance" (Acts 2:4). The word "full" in Greek means *full; complete; lacking nothing*. The believers received everything they needed to live a godly life and to launch the Church.

When we receive the baptism in the Holy Spirit, we, too, are *full, complete, and lack nothing*. God's power flows within us and comes upon us so He can do something *through* us. Jesus told His disciples to wait in Jerusalem until they were "...endued with power from on high" (Luke 24:49). The word "endued" is the Greek word *enduo*, which means *to be clothed*, and it carries *the idea of nestling into a set of clothes until you feel comfortable*.

Friend, God's intention is that you be baptized in the Holy Spirit and that you become so comfortable in His power that you begin to operate in the realm of the supernatural effortlessly. He wants you to live and function in His divine presence with ease. If you have not been baptized in the Holy Spirit and would like to be, we would be honored to join our faith with yours and pray for you to receive this precious gift. Just give us a call at 1-800-742-5593.

STUDY QUESTIONS

> **Study to shew thyself approved unto God, a workman that needeth not to be ashamed, rightly dividing the word of truth.**
> **— 2 Timothy 2:15**

1. As a believer, it is vital that you understand what makes you acceptable and in right standing with God. Carefully read Ephesians 2:1-9. Then in your own words, explain how you are saved — what part does God play and what part do you play in the process? (Also *consider* Romans 10:9,10; 2 Corinthians 5:21.)

2. Second Corinthians 3:17 (*NIV*) declares, "The Lord is the Spirit, and where the Spirit of the Lord is, there is freedom." Name some areas in your life in which you are you enjoying true freedom. These are areas where you have welcomed the Holy Spirit and have cooperated with His guidance and instruction.

3. In what areas of your life are you experiencing a lack of freedom? These are areas where you need to welcome the Holy Spirit to enter and begin His transforming work. Take a moment to surrender these to Him in prayer right now.

PRACTICAL APPLICATION

> But be ye doers of the word, and not hearers only, deceiving your own selves.
> —James 1:22

Denise shared that before she experienced the baptism in the Holy Spirit, her mind was closed to it. She had heard things about people who were Spirit-filled that really frightened her.

1. How about you? Have you heard things about Spirit-filled people or about the baptism of the Holy Spirit that have scared or confused you? If so, what have you heard?
2. How has this lesson helped dispel your fears and bring clarity on this subject?
3. If you have been baptized in the Holy Spirit, what are some of the changes He has brought about in your life since then?
4. What might your life be like without the baptism of the Holy Spirit?

LESSON 5

TOPIC
Questions About the Baptism in the Holy Spirit

SYNOPSIS

Many people have questions about the baptism in the Holy Spirit. We know from Scripture that it is real and that Jesus Himself experienced it when He was baptized in the Jordan River by John. Matthew, Mark, and Luke all say that the heavens were opened and the Spirit of God descended as a dove on Jesus and remained on Him throughout His lifetime in His earthly ministry. In fact, the baptism in the Holy Spirit is what launched Jesus into His ministry on the earth. Everything changed when the power of the Holy Spirit came, and that same amazing Person of power wants to fill every fiber of you too!

The emphasis of this lesson:

The following are solid, biblical answers to some of the most common questions asked about the baptism in the Holy Spirit.

1. Does someone have to pray for me to receive the baptism in the Holy Spirit?

You can receive the baptism in the Holy Spirit by praying alone or by having someone pray for you. It is the same as receiving Christ as your Savior: You can pray with someone at an altar in a church, or you can repent of your sin and invite Jesus into your heart on your own. In both cases of salvation and the baptism in the Holy Spirit, the location and the number of people present don't matter. The only thing needed is an open, sincere heart praying to God in faith. Like salvation, the baptism in the Holy Spirit is a work of God's grace.

2. Why should I pray in tongues?

The apostle Paul answered this question in First Corinthians 14. In verse 14, he said, "For if I pray in an unknown tongue, my spirit prayeth…." And back in verse 2, he said, "For he that speaketh in an unknown tongue speaketh not unto men, but unto God…." So when you pray in tongues, it is your spirit speaking directly to God. Jesus said, "God is a spirit…" (John 4:24). So when you pray in tongues, your spirit is speaking the language of the Spirit, which is the language of God.

There is value in praying with your understanding, but there is also great value in praying in the Spirit. Paul said, "…I will pray with the spirit, and I will pray with the understanding also: I will sing with the spirit, and I will sing with the understanding also" (1 Corinthians 14:15). When you pray in tongues, your spirit becomes fine-tuned to God's Spirit, and your mind and spirit come into agreement.

Realize that your mind is very limited. There will be times when you find yourself in situations and you will not be able to think of what to pray; your vocabulary will not be sufficient to express what needs to be said. But if you will pray in tongues with your spirit, you will bypass your mind and have an unlimited spiritual vocabulary to speak directly to God and express exactly what needs to be said in that moment. God will hear you and answer your prayer.

3. How often should I speak in tongues?

We can and should pray in tongues regularly. In First Corinthians 14:18, Paul said, "I thank my God I speak with tongues more than ye all." Paul was highly intellectual and wrote the majority of the New Testament, which has been and continues to be the doctrinal foundation of the Christian faith since its inception. He spoke in tongues often.

When Paul said, "I speak with tongues," the words "I speak" is the Greek word *lalo*, which means *I converse; I speak fluently; I speak conversationally.* This indicates that tongues was a real language to him, and he spoke it fluently. In fact, Paul said he spoke in tongues "more than ye all." The phrase "more than" is the Greek word *mallon*, which means *comparatively more*, and "ye all" means *all of you combined.* This phrase was the equivalent of Paul saying, "Compared to everyone else, I speak in tongues more than all of you combined."

Think about it. Paul said he spoke in tongues more than anyone else, and he also wrote more of the New Testament than anyone else. Thus, it could be said that the amount of divine revelation one receives from the Word is directly related to how much he or she speaks in tongues. Remember, when you speak in tongues, you speak *divine mysteries* — revelation of the Holy Spirit is released through speaking the language of the spirit (*see* 1 Corinthians 14:2).

You don't have to wait for a certain feeling to pray in tongues — "goose-bumps" are not required. Just as you don't have to feel a certain way to speak in your native tongue, you don't have to feel a certain way to speak in tongues, the language of Heaven. Just open your mouth and speak the language of the Spirit. Let prayer pour out of your spirit directly to God's Spirit, and your whole being will be empowered.

4. If I ask for the baptism in the Holy Spirit, how do I know I won't get something from the devil?

Jesus Himself answered this question in Luke 11:9 and 10:

And I say unto you, Ask, and it shall be given you; seek, and ye shall find; knock, and it shall be opened unto you. For every one that asketh receiveth; and he that seeketh findeth; and to him that knocketh it shall be opened.

While Jesus' words are a principle that applies to all areas of our lives, His words here are very specifically tied to receiving the Holy Spirit. He went on to say in Luke 11:11-13:

If a son shall ask bread of any that is a father, will he give him a stone? Or if he ask a fish, will he for a fish give him a serpent? Or if he shall ask an egg, will he offer him a scorpion? If ye then, being evil, know how to give good gifts unto your children: how much more shall your heavenly Father give the Holy Spirit to them that ask him?

Know for certain that if you ask your heavenly Father for the baptism in the Holy Spirit, He is going to give you the Holy Spirit. It's guaranteed by Jesus. You're not going to get something evil. That idea is from the enemy. He is trying to keep you from asking God for what He already wants to give you.

5. Do I have to have someone lay hands on me?

No, you don't need someone to lay hands on you to receive the baptism in the Holy Spirit. If having someone pray for you will strengthen your faith and help you receive, then ask someone to pray for you. But realize that you don't need someone to pray for you in order to receive the Spirit's infilling.

6. Is speaking in tongues a requirement for being filled with the Holy Spirit?

If you are baptized in the Holy Spirit, you are going to speak in tongues. Remember in our third lesson, we established that the book of Acts gives us a clear pattern of how God works in individuals and in the Church. In every example, when the Gospel was preached and a person surrendered their life to Christ, they were saved. They were baptized in water and in the Holy Spirit — and they spoke in tongues when they were baptized in the Holy Spirit. This is the New Testament pattern that still holds true today.

Jesus said, "…Out of the abundance of the heart [the] mouth speaks" (Luke 6:45 *NKJV*). When you are full of the Spirit in your heart, your mouth is going to give expression to what you are full of. The overflow of the Spirit will be released in the language of the Spirit — tongues are going to come out of your mouth.

7. I have prayed to be filled with the Holy Spirit, but I am having trouble getting my prayer language. Why?

If you find this to be the case for you, it is likely that your mind is getting in the way. Doubts and fears based on wrong thinking and past experiences are blocking you from experiencing all that God has for you. To overcome this obstacle, continue to feed on the truth of God's Word, especially on the truth that it is God's will to baptize you in His Holy Spirit and empower you to live victoriously. Also, keep on asking and seeking the baptism in the Holy Spirit. The truth is, God wants you to be baptized in the Holy Spirit more than you do. As you learn to rest and put your trust in Him, it will happen.

8. Can I pray in tongues silently or does it have to be out loud?

Usually, when people ask if they have to pray in tongues out loud, it is because they are timid or afraid to pray in tongues in public. Realize that in order for you speak to family members and friends, you have to speak out loud. You can't just *think* words in your mind to communicate with them. You have to open your mouth and speak, and the same is true about speaking in tongues.

Of course, if you're in a meeting or a place where you can't pray out loud, praying silently or softly under your breath is fine. However, if you can take a walk or get alone in another room and pray in the spirit out loud, it would be better.

For most of us, hearing the sound of tongues coming out of our mouths initially is very awkward. Our ears are just not used to it, and our flesh — that is, our un-renewed nature — is used to dominating us and doesn't want to relinquish its control to our re-created spirit. Nevertheless, if you will push past the uncomfortable feelings and begin praying in tongues regularly, your spirit will grow stronger, and your flesh will be put in its place.

The more you speak the language of the Spirit, the better and easier it becomes. Just begin to say to yourself, *God gave me this language. I didn't make it up, and He doesn't want me to shut up. He wants me to open my mouth and speak it out. I don't care how it sounds or how it makes me feel. I'm going to speak to God in tongues and grow in my relationship with Him.*

9. Is the infilling of the Holy Spirit something we pray for once, or is it something we have to pray for regularly?

The baptism in the Holy Spirit is something we receive *once*. We may pray a few times initially to receive this experience, but the experience itself is one time — just like salvation. After we are baptized in the Spirit, we can and should experience many *refillings*. These are times when we are in prayer, praying in tongues, and the Holy Spirit refreshes our spirit with more of Himself. We see this recorded in the pages of the book of Acts.

As you pray each day, it is a good practice to say, "Holy Spirit, fill me with more of You." Then pray in tongues, using the words He has given you. You can never exhaust God's limitless supply, and you can never have too much of His Holy Spirit.

10. Am I wrong if I pray in tongues while going about my business, or should I only pray in tongues while sitting down in prayer?

It is in your best interest — and the best interest of those you love and are in relationship with — to pray in tongues as often as you can. The Bible says, "Pray at all times (on every occasion, in every season) *in the Spirit...*" (Ephesians 6:18 *AMPC*). Think about it. When you communicate with your spouse and your children, you don't limit it to one room of the house, one day the week, for one hour. You speak to them everywhere you can, as often as you can — almost about anything and everything!

It is the same with the Holy Spirit. He desires to be your best Friend and longs to be welcome in every area of your life (*see* James 4:5). So speak in tongues, the language of the Spirit, whenever you can, wherever you can. Whether you are cooking in the kitchen, working at the office, taking a shower, driving in the car, shopping at the store, or walking in your neighborhood, open your mouth and pray with your spirit. As you do, everything about your life will improve — relationships, business transactions, personal growth — *everything!*

STUDY QUESTIONS

Study to shew thyself approved unto God, a workman that
needeth not to be ashamed, rightly dividing the word of truth.
— 2 Timothy 2:15

1. Praying in tongues is vital to your spiritual health and your effectiveness as a believer. Take a few moments to meditate on the truths found in First Corinthians 14:4 and Jude 20. In your own words, describe the rich rewards of praying in tongues that are outlined in these passages.

2. One question included in this lesson that is often asked is this: "Why should I pray in tongues?" It was then noted that the human mind is limited, and we often find ourselves in situations in which we don't know what to pray. Carefully read Romans 8:26 and 27 and explain how the Holy Spirit and the language of tongues empower you to overcome this challenge.

PRACTICAL APPLICATION

But be ye doers of the word, and not hearers only,
deceiving your own selves.
— James 1:22

1. Of the 10 questions and answers Rick covers in this lesson, which one has helped you the most at this season of life? Why is that the case?

2. Look back at your answer to Study Question 2. Have you ever experienced a situation in which you didn't know what to pray, and you prayed in the language of the Spirit? If so, briefly share what happened.

3. How did the Holy Spirit respond and go to work on your behalf — how did things begin to change for the better?

A Prayer To Receive Salvation

If you've never received Jesus as your Savior and Lord, now is the time for you to experience the new life Jesus wants to give you! To receive God's gift of salvation that can be obtained through Jesus alone, pray this prayer from your heart:

> *Jesus, I repent of my sin and receive You as my Savior and Lord. Wash away my sin with Your precious blood and make me completely new. I thank You that my sin is removed, and Satan no longer has any right to lay claim on me. Through Your empowering grace, I faithfully promise that I will serve You as my Lord for the rest of my life.*

If you just prayed this prayer of salvation, you are born again! You are a brand-new creation in Christ! Would you please let us know of your decision by going to **renner.org/salvation**? We would love to connect with you and pray for you as you begin your new life in Christ.

Scriptures for further study: John 3:16; John 14:6; Acts 4:12; Ephesians 1:7; Hebrews 10:19,20; 1 Peter 1:18,19; Romans 10:9,10; Colossians 1:13; 2 Corinthians 5:17; Romans 6:4; 1 Peter 1:3

Notes

_____

_____

_____

_____

_____

_____

_____

_____

_____

_____

_____

_____

_____

_____

_____

_____

_____

_____

_____

_____

_____

_____

_____

_____

_____

_____

_____

_____

_____

Notes

Notes

CLAIM YOUR FREE RESOURCE!

As a way of introducing you further to the teaching ministry of Rick Renner, we would like to send you FREE of charge his teaching, "How To Receive a Miraculous Touch From God" on CD or as an MP3 download.

In His earthly ministry, Jesus commonly healed *all* who were sick of *all* their diseases. In this profound message, learn about the manifold dimensions of Christ's wisdom, goodness, power, and love toward all humanity who came to Him in faith with their needs.

☑ **YES, I want to receive Rick Renner's monthly teaching letter!**

Simply scan the QR code to claim this resource or go to: **renner.org/claim-your-free-offer**

Connect
WITH US!

www.ingramcontent.com/pod-product-compliance
Lightning Source LLC
Chambersburg PA
CBHW071650040426
42452CB00009B/1825